THE
BLIND MAN'S MEAL

poems by

Peter J. Grieco

Finishing Line Press
Georgetown, Kentucky

THE
BLIND MAN'S MEAL

Copyright © 2023 by Peter J. Grieco
ISBN 979-8-88838-095-6 First Edition
All rights reserved under International and Pan-American Copyright Conventions. No part of this book may be reproduced in any manner whatsoever without written permission from the publisher, except in the case of brief quotations embodied in critical articles and reviews.

ACKNOWLEDGMENTS

Thanks to the editors of the publications in which many of these verses first appeared.

"Visible Storage," *Scholars and Rouges*.
"La gare Saint Lazare, arrivée d'un train," *Pif Magazine*
"Hypatia," *Chiron Review*
"Three Dancers in Yellow," *Kestrel*
"Angst," *The Adroit Journal*
"Boats near Åsgådstrand," *White Whale Review*
 "Interior (My Dining Room)," *The Bond Street Review*
"Le Trac." *Nexus*
"Self-Portrait," "The Casbah Gate," "Celebrations of Light," *Write from Wrong*
"Waving of Flags + Crowds," *Tiger's Eye*
"Woman, Depicted Facing and in Profile, with Glass," *Bond Street*
"Intérieur à la fenêtre ouverte," *Subtopian*
"Women Encircled by the Flight of a Bird," *Sliver of Stone Magazine*
"Triptychs," *Black Robert Journal*
"Choses Sauvages," *Loch Raven*

Publisher: Leah Huete de Maines
Editor: Christen Kincaid
Cover Art: Peter J. Grieco
Author Photo: Peter J. Grieco
Cover Design: Elizabeth Maines McCleavy

Order online: www.finishinglinepress.com
also available on amazon.com

Author inquiries and mail orders:
Finishing Line Press
PO Box 1626
Georgetown, Kentucky 40324
USA

Table of Contents

Visible Storage 1
Hunters in the Snow 2
La Gare Saint-Lazare, Arrivée D'un Train 3
Hypatia 4
Three Dancers in Yellow 5
Angst 6
The Blind Man's Meal 7
Boats Near Åsgådstrand 8
Interior (My Dining Room) 9
Artist's Room in Neulenbach 10
Le Trac 11
The Casbah Gate 12
Waving Of Flags + Crowds 13
Self-Portrait As Soldier 14
In Gray 15
Woman, Depicted Facing and in Profile, With Glass 16
The Table 17
Intérieur À La Fenêtre Ouverte 18
Women Encircled by the Flight of a Bird 19
Stenographic Figure 20
Le Baiser De L'hotel De Ville 21
On The Banks 22
Colors Arranged by Chance 23
Triptychs 24
Self-Portrait 26
Celebrations of Light 27
Choses Sauvages 28

VISIBLE STORAGE
   in the basement of the Rietberg Museum, Zürich

Sinuous bodies joining hands in Indian sandstone
ankle linked across a ledge—
Peruvian puma beside West Mexican fetishes
vermillion delicate
bone masks & rhinos of Mali
& Côte d'Ivoire—
Oblong faces of dark mystery stare
empty-eyed
longing through the glass to be touched—
Whose tongue
reaches through iron teeth to cross the aisle
from Persia, to Egypt, to Rome?
Silver bobbles, fluted bottles, feathers of a winged Isis:
I'm looking for a talisman—
& find this magic lute with its flat leather base stretched
around a hollow frame.
I imagine it to fit nicely in the player's lap.
Five strings, strung
taut, fly upward from the center
where there's a carved head serene,
for dreams to be carried off on silent waves of air.
I would capture it all
in this little bottle for you—porcelain
with painted ponies in a ring &
lion cubs at the shoulders—open the brass stopper
bring your ear to the sound!

HUNTERS IN THE SNOW
Pieter Bruegel the Elder, 1565

I was considering this picture
peering down its breakneck slope
into the village when Sasha came
with good news. Twins!
The hunt was finished. The dogs
can rest. Home & family, where
women's work is never done.
A glimpse of peace before night
returns.

Is this a scene of plenty or
of devil-may-care, despite
precarious uncertainty? The cozy
viewer playing tourist
from his armchair near the fire.
Humans have planted their flag.
The slushy streets are ground
blacker than mud.

In a dream, I
saw the short
      blocky
lines of a poem

      one
to four words long
veering from
the throbbings of passion

to the commerce of
      friendship
from the sharing of
      ease

to the comforts
of laughter, the
miracles of life
      twice answered.

LA GARE SAINT-LAZARE, ARRIVÉE D'UN TRAIN
Monet, 1877

Corot wrote, "Nothing has value except
in our hunger for what seizes us."
But hunger can be but a vague yearning,
inarticulate as confused mist, obscure as
steaming plumes of smoke & suffocating
fog, overwhelming, with so much muchness.
One hunger competes with another. One
train arrives, another parts. I can't get
my head above the clouds. On my tiptoes I
rise to meet your eyes. Yes, at last I am
certain. It must be you, both arriving &
departing, both the sharp spike taken to
the heart of perception & the answering thrust
aimless in every direction. Hear those
churning engines, unmistakable even
in the dark, calling for images instead
of a muddle of adjectives?

HYPATIA
Charles William Mitchel, 1885

"Fables should be taught as fables" is one
of the fabulous dicta pinned to Hypatia
by tradition. As for images, there
are three tableaux: She lectures her elders;
She chastens her suitors; She resists
her murderers. Poets, painters,
& chroniclers, from Byzantines through
Gibbon, Kingsley, & Mitchel, have wanted
to sing her praises & do her honor: but she
seems only to feed their nostalgia for the
last pure days of Antiquity or inflame
their Amazonian fantasies of female
domination, for which they will turn
tables & rend her white flesh to rags.

Hypatia, our teacher, made the streets
of Alexandria an academy, trailing
graybeards behind her ambiguously,
gothic arches bridging Venetian canals
beneath her feet, a halo adorning
her golden hair: a Greek martyred by Christians,
by them resuscitated as a Christian
martyr, just as Holy Wisdom is butchered
to trim St. Mark's. Her would-be lover was
a boy, her student. She cured him with the
music of the spheres.

But she never really
cured him. "Take these bloody rags! Am I not
repugnant?" He consulted Pythagoras
& returned the next day, insisting she
was not. There is something not there about
Hypatia. In the chronicles the
ringleader of Cyril's mob of monks who
came to smoke her is identified as
Peter, against whom she "rose for one moment
to her full height, naked, snow-white"
to no avail.

THREE DANCERS IN YELLOW
Degas, 1891

We want in our cynicism to be told
that these ladies are not
as fresh & pretty as they appear—
that they curse & spit & smell
but our eyes tell us, no.
It is not irony that Degas
has made them so sumptuously rich
dressing them in ruby, in gold,
in sapphire, & if they are just girls, after all
dancers working their trade, that trade
is to bring illusion & grace to a left-footed world.
Standing at the wings backstage, one adjusts
her taffeta costume as another slakes
the kind of thirst we see nowadays
in cola commercials. The third pivots
with habitual, almost bored, precision.
She has broken frame as in a photograph.
Some say they are all the same girl
that what we see is a rapid sequence
& not an arrested moment held
in great suspense. I want it both ways:
I want them held
there—however many they may be—
& I want them desperately
in the next moment to re-join the rush
that blurs in dazzlement around them.

ANGST
Edvard Munch, 1896

One in black, one in blood red,
these prints flow together

like shapes in the stream—night
& day, I suppose, the faces

always waiting. Faces in a crowd
where no crowd ought to gather

at the tip of some soggy wilderness, vibrating
with the shock of life, of living,

or of having lived. There is a town
in the distance—but they have come far—

if from there—to beckon. See the lights?
See the lights? The great waves

shimmering overhead like the hand of . . .

THE BLIND MAN'S MEAL
    Pablo Picasso, 1903

For Rilke, the subject matter of a painting becomes
    "no longer 'simply' what is pictured

        but also the effect that
    follows from how the picturing is done."

The blind man reaches with his fingertips—
    his "eyes"—for the only red object

        on a plane of blue:
    "a densely quilted, ancient Egyptian shadow-blue."

In this same way, we reach to taste
    the music that is the blind man's bread.

BOATS NEAR ÅSGÅDSTRAND
Edvard Munch, 1904

This is what it looked like
stepping out on those slippery
rocks that line the strand. But I
didn't see it till I said it, while
discussing Boccaccio's Middle Ages
& my own, how close she came
to my own perception, following
each other into the depth & distance.
Both of us were sure to drown
that way. Yet here by the shore,
all seemed safe. We took each
other's hands & waded out a few
steps upon those shapely rocks that
scoured our feet, surrounded by a sun
blinding swell of light. A few steps
on, we bobbed & laughed, drawn
to what some call the brink.

INTERIOR (MY DINING ROOM)
Kandinsky, 1909

Colors are mischievous souls—fickle,
promiscuous, "ready at any moment
to mingle." K was rather like that himself,
a chameleon of Europe in an age
when Europe was still like that itself—
with fluid borders that railways & steamships
made porous—spurring great movements
of peoples that took unprecedented wars
to clamp down on. K was set in motion
with a Russian tea merchant's legacy
that landed him a home & garden in Murnau,
& a rented townhouse in Munich.
Münter did her own *Interior* the same year,
depicting rooms of their Murnau house.
You can see K in bed at the back,
sitting up with a book. The window is dark;
a warm light glows from within.
She has brushed in a jolly runner, angled
along the bright floor planking, leading
to the cool blue of their room. *Innerlich*—
a sense of being "suffused with inward life"—
is the quality these painters worked towards.
It was that life, not visible objects,
that they aimed at, "paintings without objects"—
seeing past the *äusserlichkeit* of conventional
recognition. That's why in this room the
radiator is that unheard of color, why the wall
paper glows so, & the table vibrates, why
the shining shield adorning the sideboard
is no longer either china or pewter, why
nothing looks empty or abandoned. The room
has absorbed its aura & pays it back
in perpetuity.

ARTIST'S ROOM IN NEULENBACH
Egon Schiele, 1911

This still-life invites a song,
for what sister arts all share
is the doing, the performance,
the act. What he made—dabbing
paint one handed, scraping it off
with the other, regarding his *chambre
à coucher* while he poses, balanced
at the threshold just inside its door frame,
a man on stage in his underwear juggling
a conception against what may achieve it—
I imitate by rough analogy, to please
& then to bed.

                Yet more than Schiele
in the act, who left at length this
quiet trace; no, not the artist painting,
but the life inside this room—here
is my song. It is just so. We approach
this picture from a distance, as if home
from long travels we see again our
own poor lodgings transfigured, & more
vibrantly our own than we'd remembered
when first setting out, & other intentions
intervened. The table in the corner
propped just so to flatter the eye,
objects exactly where I'd forgotten
I'd left them miraculously surviving intact
& coming slowly unfrozen in time.

LE TRAC
Matisse at the window

Total pictorial intensity, the stage
set for expression, the wave
held up for all to see—a circus balance
of will & feeling, the broken
flow of dancers, tables arranged with crystal
& oranges, colors exchanging lines
of force like lovers in a lazy luxury of desire:
Form from within, worked & re-worked,
until I look at last upon my own mind:
until all I see & the world I move in aspire
to be one of my pictures. The blank
canvas easeled by the window awaits again
energy of eyes' urge for hand to answer.
See how it trembles! The Seine
a plane of light, the church above the bridge,
all a bleeding blue. Ah! but not
the piercing blue of Nice, for where
is the star-bright splash of Icarus?
the tiger's strip? An image—that's all
I am to you! I tell her she doesn't understand.
An image is expression, the form intuition
takes, creates, the refined performance of all I feel
& know of thee. She opposes me, my nerves
are bad, my voice stutters. I'm stuffy as a lawyer
in this shirt tonight. Shall I strip, paint my body
blue & roll across the scissors?

THE CASBAH GATE
Matisse, 1912

That ghost, again, Ayşe—there,
just now—in the corner—do you see her?
Nay—it's a trick of the sun.
Come back to your needle work.
Every stitch is a credit
towards heaven. So the women
flash their needles, white
in the blue shadows of the harem.
The door beyond the door
is open for traders to call—all the
riffraff of the dusty city, Tangier
& the sharp morning strikes
at the sides of the passage
& a crimson stain spreads
through the tall keyhole
of the Casbah Gate.

WAVING OF FLAGS + CROWDS
Giacomo Balla, 1915

Under the laws of synaesthesia
we have the "Painting of Sounds,
Noises, & Smells," where the senses
speak for each other in many different
languages. Colors of the cubists are in
washed out French, while putrid noses
sniff at corners in narcotic Latin
& common touch sounds roughly
German. Oh, how the taste of the world
salts itself Icelandic & finds
seasoning in the blood of Turks
& Kurds. Ears whisper Sicilian Vespers
& the voice of human anguish chortles
Milanese over the dark lake. It's 1915
& while some painters have fled to Zurich
or New York others take sides according
to their nationalities. I can almost
hear the joyous music & hurrahs in Balla's
commentary on the scene, this spectacle
of mass feeling soaring, everything
seeming to float & flow. The harsh, true
colors of the flag strewn canvas billow
with energy above softer pastels, so light
hearted & free. Notice, however, how
all the curved lines come to points &
that the whole turns out to be
less than a foot wide by nine inches
high. There must be a sixth sense
written in Chinese, backwards across
the sand of an Asian steppe.

SELF-PORTRAIT AS SOLDIER
Ernst Ludwig Kirchner, 1915

Patrick Joyce's study showed
how the rise of the factory system
in the English Midlands—in places
like Ashton, Stalybridge, & Blackburn—
produced "working-class consent
& subordination." The next step
was war—society rushing head-long
into self-mutilation. Kirchner was
among the complicit but conflicted.
Instead of "suffering transformed into art,"
here was art turned to suffering
& reduced to self-mockery.
The gangrened stub
tickling the model's inner thigh
with phantom brush strokes—
the painter in the uniform of his
own repression. Last year,
there were over 208 military suicides
each lone soldier desperate to withdraw
consent.

IN GRAY
Kandinsky, 1919

I'd like to imagine this picture hanging
on the wall beside my bed
so I could study its patterns daily
as I did with the paisley curtains
that hung in my boyhood room.
No need to ask the meaning of abstraction
when I could follow the flowing rhythms
in half-dreams lost to nascent, objectless
desire. How my thoughts would scheme
& sport along the curves, & pool in pockets,
or collect in eddies, forgetting all
source in care or question—till a summer
breeze dispersed them. From long habit
I would know these lines & shapes, too—see
the naked torso, the letters flung in air,
& the gateway arch beneath which
whimsical craft steer towards
a sun poised to vanish. K believed
an artist must strive beyond the forms
of nature to free the spirit, & it is tempting
to read these wild canvases as allegories
of personal & social possibility. This kind
of work upset Stalinists & Fascists alike.
Already there were calls for
"new order" in painting—but before
he ditched Moscow, K conjured this paradise.
"The end of my dramatic period,"
he later thought. That's why I need
this painting next to me a while longer,
to watch its forms compete, to see the air
let out of hopes, to see them fill again,
to feel it spark back to life in early
morning light, looming, unfinished.

WOMAN, DEPICTED FACING AND IN PROFILE, WITH GLASS
Jean Metzinger, 1919

The more I gaze
across the table
the fonder I grow
of you, my dear.
Not dualism—
yes, no—
oscillation—fusion
perhaps I shall.
Not only back-&-forth
but in-&-out. Enfolding
your drink, your arms
as we might each other.
Speckles, squares.
Lines, squiggles.
My dark bright lady,
turn again towards me!

THE TABLE
Pierre Bonnard, 1925

She sits at the edge of the table
& floats to the front of the mind
in this context of good things
of baskets & breakfasts, the "accretion"
of meals & moments, olives, buns, coffee
raisins, of the painter—brooding
is exactly the wrong word—chewing
over each accent of thought & sense
the blazing white cloth a canvas
of dancing blue & cutting crimson. Still
she is soft & full, fleecy, ready
to look up & giggle, were she not
so absorbed in her task. But call her
&—it seems—her voice will answer.

It is as when night folds round the sleeper
arranging contents of his day, spreading
all before him, unhurried, from all
to choose, as if taste were music
singing lullabies, no Brussels sprouts in sight
& knives & forks were the tools of soldiers who
have laid down arms at last, while
the starry sky steals through cracks
in the creaking pea-green sward.

Ah, "bourgeois fairyland" of "idleness &
reverie"—Bonnard's daily walk those
youthful years in Paris, "waiting for
that sudden welling-up of excited
recognition" that evokes the meeting
of eyes. But what if the excited moment
came with a lazy eye & you were looking
the wrong way? What if you were absent
at the essential moment of seeing? What
then can memory recover? Yet out of the corner
of perception—she returns—nor
has she moved from beyond the shifting
round of expectation & approximations—
jolting to awareness.

INTÉRIEUR À LA FENÊTRE OUVERTE
Raoul Dufy, 1928

A frightened goose suddenly aware of danger, & rousing the whole flock with its cries, does not tell the others what it has seen but contaminates them with its fear. So it is with the mass-production of "pseudo Dufys." Still, a well-painted turnip is more significant than a poorly painted Madonna. When Dufy left Ecole des Beaux-Arts he was convinced instruction more hindrance than help & deliberately switched to his untrained left hand. He wanted to express "not what I see, but what exists for me, my reality." Only in this way, by ruthless simplification, does communication become possible. For the experience that exists for each individual consciousness is, strictly speaking, not communicable. Anxiety. Pacing the floor. Looking out one window then the next. Back & forth. Blue & Red. Chairs where no one sits. Then the plunge to the plage.

WOMEN ENCIRCLED BY THE FLIGHT OF A BIRD
Jean Miró, 1941

These are the stars of night
scratched into a shell by *Homo erectus.*

This is the strength we seek
from the ground we walk on—just as a tree is fed
through its roots.

These are the women who
by skirting trauma have broken free

& the bird that
arouses their departure,

stenciled vivisections of shapes,
fragments painted on the wrappings of
mummies.

STENOGRAPHIC FIGURE
Jackson Pollock, 1941

Awareness
amidst a field
of stimuli
a vaguer sense
pressing upon us
particulars imposing
on particulars
outside
the bounds of habit &
social constraint
automatism
resolving into
an emergent sum—

Have you got that?

LE BAISER DE L'HOTEL DE VILLE
Robert Doisneau, 1950

recurrence
in this staged photograph
over time
reducing the complexity
the next element
to shades of grey
arriving
caught up in the irrationality of the crowd
within sight or earshot
striving for the general good
of the previous, so that
rather than for individual advantage
you feel in the midst
on the other hand
of a movement
le spectacle gratuit
carried along

ON THE BANKS
Robert Doisneau, 1951

Doesn't this sort of photography involve
manipulation? Always. *Blanc et noir.*
Positioning for light. For aperture.
Then, too, we'll never know if the figures
were posed. Actors? Aren't we all? The utterly
ordinary can be marvelous, but
it must be, as you say, manipulated
by imagination. Time does the rest.
Their sun has caught the biceps of a handsome
boy threading a fishhook, his legs dangling
the concrete embankment a few feet above
where meanders the Seine, her forehead kissed
by the same luminosity. They sit back-
to-back, almost without touching. That's
what I find so provocative, so telling, so well
imagined. Who has said what to encourage
them to lean together like that, as if shoulders
did the listening, as well as the hearing?
Merde! His calloused fingers poke unsuccessfully
at the lure. By contrast she's all smiles,
softness & sureness, not needing to look down
at the knitting she has brought, as if the artist has
given back to us the conversation
we had last Wednesday.

COLORS ARRANGED BY CHANCE
Ellsworth Kelly, 1951

Is this "what art looks like when it turns its
back on nature . . . anti-memetic, anti-
real"? Colors, chance, arrangement.
What's unnatural about that? O'Hara wanted
poetry, like modern painting, to be an activity
"which liberates certain forces . . . permits
them to emerge upon the void of silence,"
as opposed to seeking "some preconceived idea
or perception."

His poems come scattered with, piled
with, references to known people,
records of overheard conversations, evocations
of particular experiences, as he sought to "transmute
life into art . . ." defamiliarization that
necessarily refers to the familiar.

Have Kelly's colors ever been arranged
quite this way? Like Jupiter & Mars hung high
in a pre-dawn sky?

TRIPTYCHS
Milton Rogovin, 1994

The artist's aims have changed
since the first series of shots when
he couldn't resist the desire
for transfiguration—why should he?—
by eliciting the eloquence of light
the grain in wood, each brick
of a graffitied facade, arranging
Madonna & Child couplings, offsetting
solitary rebels. Balance—Contrast—
Gentle Irony—Depth of Focus—
all help to unmask dignity
in simple passions, neglected
beauties, vitality amid ruin, *Miller
High Life* captioned above
the granite resolve of the poor.

A parent staggers out of a darkened
stairwell to sun on a broken
step. Velvet painted peacocks
framing a lace draped mantle
behind a doll-like tiara-ed Virgin
express the same simple optimism
& innocent trust that a small girl
does, clinging about her proud
father's waist. A self-contained
immigrant family gazes expectantly
at the camera proclaiming, We Are Here.

A Mod Squad in turtlenecks, shades
& hooped earrings, like a scene out of *Hair*
steps over the color line to groove
with one another. The artist provokes
a silent language, musters a patience
to hear where there is literally nothing
to be heard, so that it is we who fumble

to speak, we who want to shout our
sympathy, our respect & solidarity, even
our admiration, for those from whom
did we actually hear their guttural voices
we might turn away in distaste.

By the third group of images
this glamour is not even attempted.
Where are the pan pipes, the bare chests
& subtle toes—a *ménage à trois* with dog
ready for the April morning? Where are
the tight groups & couples, the solitary
souls brave in the light, the high school
girl with pencil in her teeth, fire
in her hair? Replaced, often, by ungainly
families, elders whose dreams have
vanished, kids who look spoiling
for a fight. Simultaneity lapses
inevitably into sequence, a rhythm
of cycles, narratives of loss. Tragic
stasis unwinds in bitter folly. Distracted
by this progression, the camera loses
its eye for detail & compositions give
way to a chaos closer to real life.

SELF-PORTRAIT
Alan E. Cober, 1997

Wind whistles through centuries waking devils—
the wind rattles through walls
shaking down a turbulence of images.
This ruddy, bulbous nose
my ears, senses, eyes, hands—
the flesh of me feels deceptively moored & stable
but I spin in a vortex.
You spin in one, too. Though I show the same face
as the moon, I belong only to the vanishing
instant. I am already my own cadaver.
The calm behind these supple brows is alert
to that certain prophesy.
The wind has bleached the light
spits rain, creates floods, unearths bones—
slits open the brown valley.
How soon these pigments perish. They fade
as does your own seeing.

CELEBRATIONS OF LIGHT
Various painters, 2002

Watercolorists try harder.
But the titles that they give
can sometimes seem amateurish
for fauve cows & photo realism.
"Moonstruck" stretches its rigging
across a silent sea groaning to the pull
of taut forces. Scenes of Venice abound
in "Reflections" & one more "Evening's Last Glow."
These conventional ambitions respond well
to *alla prima*, wet on wet, masking,
& stretching, beguiling us with "negative
painting." "A Roma" is a pun on perfume
pinned to a study of shimmering decanters
of nickel & glass. "Face to Face" brings us
nose-to-nose with a grand-fatherly bull,
presumably toothless. Goodbye to summer
& unkept promises. Pears & stripes forever.
"Innocence Lost" shows us the cat that
ate the canary. "Make Mine Peppermint"
is the one that drew me in, to sit under
one of its red umbrellas, to wait, but nothing
happens. She doesn't come. "Time
Stands Still" arrests a guttering candle.
"School's Out" seems blind to irony:
these fish will never escape.

CHOSES SAUVAGES
> *Alice in Wonderland depicted in a shop window*

The woman who designs these scenes
dyes her hair black with wide streaks of
color, maroon one month, orange the next.
Though she studied as a goldsmith,
she doesn't make any of the jewelry.
Instead, she clerks, & she decorates
(for Halloween, she scissored shells
of clementines into shrunken pumpkin
heads), & she assembles these wide-eyed
window displays that never fail to
captivate the crowd coming out of Kuni's.
If fantasy & ornament are at one
of the wild poles of our history, sheer
inarticulate passion is at the other.

Nor are novices the only ones that make
these mistakes, confusing *sauver* & *sauvage*,
to rescue the wild things, to be rescued
by them. The same with horses & hair.
My Korean students mixed up awkward
& squid, in Ankara it was lion & snake.
These little misunderstandings keep piling up.
"Use your words," a father prompts
his stymied daughter, as if they alone could pull
her from the well. "Use your words."

Here there is a table set out under a tree,
Alice, the Hatter, & the Hare,
in the company of an ink black raven,
& a writing desk appointed in jade.
"I always say what I mean," she insists.
You might as well say, "I get what I like!"
Being half crazy isn't crazy enough. Move
one place over &, the perpetual party continues.

Next time, we'll sit in your garden, Emilie
surrounded by May roses & ask Pampinea
to tell one of *her* stories. As evening falls,
some of the ladies will want to dance
to songs wild hearts sing.

Peter J. Grieco grew up in Buffalo, NY. He earned a doctorate in English from SUNY Buffalo, completing his thesis on the sociolinguistics of workingclass poetry while working as a school bus driver. After teaching literature and language at universities in Ankara and Seoul, he taught English composition for many years at Buffalo area colleges. His poems have been widely published in small magazines on-line and in print. His blog "At the Musarium and Other Writings" [https://pjgrieco.wordpress.com/] archives much of this work. His chapbooks include *Réception Donnée Chez un Riche Marchand Arabe* (Underground Books, 2018) and *At the Musarium: A Virtual Chapbook* (dispatchespoetrywars.com, 2019).

www.ingramcontent.com/pod-product-compliance
Lightning Source LLC
Chambersburg PA
CBHW022126090426
42743CB00008B/1031